The Camcorder Thief

By Richard Brown

Series Editor: Louis Fidge

Contents

1. Robert's camcorder — 3
2. The children make a model — 7
3. The man in the black jacket — 11
4. The pickpocket — 15
5. On the Big Wheel — 20
6. Who stole the camcorder? — 23
7. An emergency at the airport — 27
8. The children are on TV — 31
9. In the camera shop — 35
10. The surprise parcel — 39

The Fun Fair — 42
People who work in TV — 44

Chapter 1
Robert's camcorder

'When's Robert coming?' Steven asked.

'Soon,' said Mum.

'What time is he coming?' Sarah asked.

'Very soon,' said Dad.

Steven and Sarah loved Robert's visits. Robert was their big cousin.

The children waited on the balcony of their apartment for an hour. Then –

'Look, there he is!' Steven shouted.

'Hello! How are you?' said Robert, as the children opened the door.

'Fine,' said Sarah.

'Fine,' said Steven.

Robert put his bag on the table.

'I've got a surprise for you,' he said, with a smile. 'Can you guess what I've got in my bag?'

The children shook their heads.

'Close your eyes,' said Robert.

'OK, now you can open them.'

'A camcorder! Wow! That's great!' said Steven.

'How does it work?' Sarah asked.

'You press this button,' Robert said,
'and you look at this screen.
I'll film something today to show you.
Then I'll put it on a DVD
and you can watch the film on TV.'

'Can you film me playing football?' Steven asked.

'OK,' said Robert,
'if you try to score some exciting goals!'

That afternoon, Robert ran up and down
next to the football pitch with his camcorder.
He filmed Steven and his friends as they played football.

Later, it was exciting to watch the film on TV.

Chapter 2
The children make a model

'I'm going to put on a fashion parade with my friends,' Sarah told Robert. 'Can you film it, please?'

'OK!' said Robert.

So Sarah and her friends put on a fashion parade in the apartment.

Robert pressed the zoom button on his camcorder and filmed them close up.

Then he played the film.
Everyone laughed and pointed at themselves on the TV.

'Do you think Dad will let **us** have a camcorder?' Steven asked his sister.

'Let's ask him,' Sarah replied.

Dad shook his head.
'No. You are too young,' he said,
'and camcorders are too expensive.'

So the children made a model camcorder, instead.
They covered the model with silver foil.

When it was finished, it looked great.

Outside, the children pretended to be a TV film crew.

Sarah interviewed a neighbour who was cleaning her windows.

Steven filmed her with the model camcorder.

Next, they interviewed a cyclist. His bike had a flat tyre.

Just then, a young man walked up the street towards them.

As the man walked past them,
Steven pretended to film him.

The man was wearing a black jacket,
with a picture of a tiger on the back.

'I like your jacket,' said Sarah.

But the man wasn't very friendly.
He stopped and walked back towards Sarah and Steven.
He looked angry.

Chapter 3
The man in the black jacket

'Don't point that thing at me!' the man demanded.

'Sorry,' said Steven. 'I was only filming you.'

'I don't like people filming me,' said the man. 'You should ask first.'

'But it isn't a **real** camcorder,' said Sarah. 'We were only pretending.'

'Don't answer back!' said the man.

The man pointed at the model camcorder.
'**I've** got a **real** camcorder at home,' he said.

'So has our cousin Robert,' Sarah replied.

'Oh?' said the man. Suddenly, he was interested.

'What's your camcorder like?' Steven asked.
'Does it record on DVD?'

'Does it have a zoom button?' Sarah asked.

'Of course,' he said.
'It's the best camcorder you can buy.'

The children thought he was boasting.
'We don't believe you,' said Steven.

Then the man looked even more angry.
The children were frightened, and ran off.

The man watched them run back to their apartment.

He saw Robert on the balcony.
Robert was filming a plane in the sky.

When Robert pointed the camcorder
at the man in the black jacket, he walked away quickly.

The next day, Robert was filming in the street.
A car drove up fast behind him.
It was going straight towards him.

Suddenly, a hand came out of the car window and tried to take the camcorder.

Steven saw everything from the balcony.
'Look out!' he shouted.

Robert jumped out of the way, just in time.

The car raced off.

Chapter 4
The pickpocket

Steven ran down to see if Robert was hurt.

'That car nearly ran me down!' said Robert, as he got up slowly.

'The driver tried to take your camcorder. Did you see?' Steven asked.

'No, I didn't,' Robert replied.
'Thank you for shouting.
As a reward, I'm going to lend you my camcorder.
I'll show you how to use it.'

Steven jumped up and down in excitement.
'That's great!' he said.

The next day Steven made his first film.

His dad had a shop in the mall.
He sold watches and jewellery.
Steven decided to make a film about the shop.

Sarah interviewed Dad and Steven filmed them.

'What do you like about your shop?' Sarah asked.

'I like talking to the customers
and selling them nice things,' Dad said.

Steven filmed a customer as she bought
one of Dad's most expensive watches.

He kept filming as she put the watch in her pocket,
and walked out of the shop.

But then something strange happened.

The man in the black jacket appeared again.
He bumped into the customer.
Steven saw that he did it on purpose.

'Oh – I'm very sorry,' said the man.

At the same time, another man quickly took the new watch from the woman's pocket.

'Stop, thief!' Steven shouted. 'Stop that pickpocket!'

Dad ran out of the shop, and grabbed the pickpocket. The pickpocket struggled, but Dad did not let go of him.

'That man took my watch,' the woman said.

'The watch is mine. I bought it. Let me go!' said the pickpocket.

'He's lying,' said Steven.
'And I can prove it. I filmed it all.'

'The other man ran away,' said Dad.
'They must work together.'

The woman telephoned the police.

'Let's film a report,' said Sarah.

So Steven filmed her as she described the robbery.
Then she interviewed the woman.

When the police arrived,
Steven showed them his film of the robbery
and the police arrested the pickpocket.

The police asked Dad to send them a copy of the DVD.

That evening, the family watched the children's report.

'That was very good!' said Dad proudly.

Chapter 5
On the Big Wheel

The next day, Steven and Sarah wanted to make another film.

'I know – let's film the amusement park,' said Steven.

'That sounds like fun,' said Robert.

At the park, Sarah interviewed people as they got off the Big Wheel. They were happy and excited.

'I want to go on the Big Wheel too,' said Sarah.

'I'll come with you,' said Robert.

'And I'll film you,' said Steven.

None of them noticed the man in the black jacket.
He was in charge of the Big Wheel.
He made it start and stop.

He saw Steven, and he saw Robert's camcorder.
He wanted the camcorder more than anything!

Suddenly, the Big Wheel stopped turning.
Everyone thought it was broken.

A girl on the Big Wheel began to cry.

A boy shouted, 'I want to get off!'

A woman said, 'Call the fire service!'

Steven filmed it all. He was so pleased that something exciting was happening!

Then suddenly, a hand covered his eyes, and someone grabbed the camcorder from his hands.

Chapter 6
Who stole the camcorder?

The thief pushed Steven to the ground.
Steven heard someone running away,
but he did not see the thief.
He got up and shouted, 'Stop, thief!'

But the thief had disappeared.

'Someone stole Robert's camcorder,' Steven thought.
'He'll be so upset.'

Steven ran round the amusement park.
He looked for the thief with the camcorder.
He felt like crying.

A few minutes later, the man in the black jacket went back to the Big Wheel.
He did not have the camcorder with him.
He pressed a button, and the Big Wheel started turning again.

Everyone was pleased to get off the ride safely.
Steven quickly found Robert and Sarah,
and told them what had happened.

Robert **was** upset about his camcorder.
But he was more worried about Steven.
'Are you OK?' he asked.

Steven nodded.

Robert called the police on his mobile phone.
Steven told them about the robbery.

At home, they watched the evening news. There was a report about the emergency at the amusement park.

'Look!' Sarah shouted suddenly. She pointed at the TV screen. 'It's him!'

'Who?' said Steven.

'The man in the black jacket,' she replied. 'The man who nearly ran Robert down in the car. The man who helped the pickpocket. He was there in the amusement park!'

'Are you sure?' Mum asked. 'Lots of people wear black jackets.'

'Not with a tiger on!' said Sarah.

Robert phoned the police again.

The police returned to the amusement park.
They questioned the man in the black jacket.
They searched his car.
They found the camcorder in the back of the car.

They found a lot of other stolen things too.

The police arrested the man,
and gave the camcorder back to Robert.

Everyone was very happy.

Chapter 7
An emergency at the airport

'Let's interview Steven about the robbery,' said Robert to Sarah. 'I'll film you.'

'How did you feel when the thief covered your eyes?' Sarah asked Steven.

'I felt angry,' said Steven. 'And very brave.'

'Really?' said Sarah. 'Did you fight back?'

'Like a tiger,' said Steven.

'Then why did he get away?'

'He was twice as big as me,' said Steven. 'It was like fighting with a bear.'

Robert looked at Sarah and she smiled.

The next day the family drove to the airport.
It was time for Robert to go home.

Steven filmed the planes as Robert waited for his plane.

Suddenly he said, 'Hey, look at this!'

A plane was making an emergency landing.
One of its wings was on fire.

The emergency services rushed to the plane as soon as it stopped moving.

'Keep filming, Steven,' said Sarah.

As Steven filmed, Sarah reported what was happening.

'There is a lot of smoke coming from the wing,' she said. 'The passengers are sliding down the chute. It must be very frightening, but everyone looks calm.'

Steven used the zoom button to get a close-up of the fire and smoke and of the passengers hurrying to safety.

'It looks like everyone is OK,' said Sarah.
'The fire service is putting out the fire.
Look at that huge cloud of black smoke over the runway!'

'This is so exciting!' said Steven.

Chapter 8
The children are on TV

When the emergency was over, Dad said,
'Well done, Sarah and Steven.
That was excellent reporting.
I've got an idea …'

He called the TV studio on his mobile phone.

'Hello? Is that the TV studio?' he said.
'Have you heard about the emergency at the airport?
Well, my children filmed it on a camcorder.
Do you want to see their film?'

The people at the TV studio were very excited.
'Come at once,' they said.

When the family arrived at the TV studio,
a famous newsreader shook their hands.

Lots of TV people came to see the children's film.
They clapped when they saw it.

The producer of the evening news said,
'We'll show some of your film tonight.
Well done! You're very talented!'

'But first we have to interview **you**,' said the producer.

'Why?' said Sarah.

'Because you're part of the story.
Now, you need to get ready.'

So a make-up woman put make-up on their faces, combed their hair, and made them look tidy.

Then the famous newsreader interviewed them about their airport emergency film.

In all the excitement, Robert missed his plane.
He decided to go home the next day.

That evening, they all watched
the children's report on TV.

They gasped when they saw the plane's wing on fire.

They were quiet when they saw
the frightened passengers.

'You both did very well,' said Dad.
'Like a real cameraman and a real reporter.'

They watched their interview.
It was fantastic!

Chapter 9
In the camera shop

The next morning, Mum and Dad were whispering.

'What's the big secret?' Sarah demanded.

'We're going shopping for something,' said Mum. 'And you are both coming, to help us choose it.'

'Choose what?' said Steven.

'Wait and see,' said Dad.

'But I think you'll like it,' said Mum with a smile.

As Steven and Sarah walked into town with their parents, some people recognised them from the TV.

'Well done,' they said.
'Your report was excellent.'

The children felt very proud, and very happy.

'Well, here we are,' said Dad, at last.

They were outside a camera shop.
There were lots of camcorders in the window.

'Let's go in and look around,' said Dad.

Steven and Sarah had a wonderful time in the shop.
They looked at every camcorder.
Their favourite one was yellow.

'OK – it's time to go home now,' said Mum.

Steven and Sarah were disappointed.

'Aren't we going to buy one?' Sarah asked.

'But you said …' Steven began.

'Excuse me,' said Dad.
'I've got to make a phone call.'

'Hello,' he said. 'Is that the TV studio?'

He walked away. The children could not hear what he was saying.

They were very puzzled.

Chapter 10
The surprise parcel

That evening, the family drove to the airport again to say goodbye to Robert.

'I don't want to go home,' he said.
'When Steven and Sarah are around,
there's always something exciting happening!
Call me, when your next adventure begins.'

'As long as you bring your camcorder,' said Steven.
'We're going to miss it.'

The family waited until Robert's plane took off.
Then they drove home.

The next morning, a parcel arrived.
It was addressed to Steven and Sarah.

'Can we open it?' they asked.

'Eat your breakfast first,' said Mum.
'And clean your teeth.'

They ate their breakfast quickly.
They cleaned their teeth quickly.
They wanted to see what was in the parcel.

'Can we open it now?' Sarah asked.

Dad nodded and smiled.

Inside the parcel was a smart, yellow camcorder, just like their favourite one in the shop.

There was a note with it.

'For Steven and Sarah,' the note said.
'From everyone at the TV studio.
Film some more exciting stories for us!'

'Wow!' the children said.

'What do you want to film first?' asked Sarah, excitedly.

'Oh, anything!' said Steven.
'Something interesting will happen …
it always does when **we** start filming!'

The Fun Fair

Round about
And round about
And round about we go.
Around the merry roundabout
We're riding high and low.
Our prancing horses leap and bound
And gallop high above the ground
As round about
And round about
And round about we go.

Swinging in the swingboat,
Swinging as we go;
Swinging, swinging, swinging,
High and then low.
Swinging to the cloudy sky,
High, low, high,
Swinging to the ground below,
Low, high, low.

The gleaming world begins to reel
As upwards steals the great Big Wheel.
We're slowly lifted through the air,
Until we see the seething Fair,
The stalls, the swings, the streaming people.
Fields and trees, and distant steeple.

Isabel Best

People work in many different TV jobs. Together they make the programmes you watch on television.

Producer

A producer thinks of good ideas for programmes. He or she finds the director, scriptwriters, and actors for a programme.

Director

The director is in charge of filming the programme, and must decide what it will look like when it is finished.

Scriptwriter

When a programme tells a story, scriptwriters write the words for the actors to say.

Sometimes they write news reports, too.

Actor

Actors pretend to be different characters, to act out a story. They must be good at remembering their words.

Camera operator

The pictures we see on the TV are filmed by camera operators.

They must understand how to get the pictures the director wants.

Sound recordist

The voices and other sounds that go with the pictures are recorded by a sound recordist.

Reporters

For news programmes, a good reporter is very important. He or she tells us what is happening. A reporter must look smart and speak clearly.

Make-up artist

Actors, reporters, and people being interviewed need to be 'made up' so they look good on TV. Make-up artists and hair stylists do this job.

Macmillan Education
4 Crinan Street
London N1 9XW
A division of Macmillan Publishers Limited
Companies and representatives throughout the world

ISBN 978-1-4050-6011-0

Text © Richard Brown, 2006
Design and illustration © Macmillan Publishers Limited 2006

First published 2006

All rights reserved; no part of this publication may be reproduced, stored in a retrieval system, transmitted in any form, or by any means, electronic, mechanical, photocopying, recording, or otherwise, without the prior written permission of the publishers.

Design and layout by Anthony Godber
Illustrated by Jean de Lemos and Theresa Tibbetts
Cover design by Linda Reed & Associates
Cover illustration by Jean de Lemos

The authors and publishers would like to thank the following for permission to reproduce their photographic material:
Alamy pp45, 46(t), 47(t), Photodisc Red pp44(t),
Superstock pp46(b), Taxi pp44(b)

The Series Editor and the Author would like to give special thanks to Gill McLean for her contribution in setting up the *Macmillan Explorers* series, for her continuous encouragement, and for her positive and practical help and advice throughout its production.

Although we have tried to trace and contact copyright holders before publication, in some cases this has not been possible. If contacted we will be pleased to rectify any errors or omissions at the earliest opportunity.

Printed and bound in Malaysia

2016
13